DIGITAL AND INFORMATION LITERACY ™

NETIQUETTE
A STUDENT'S GUIDE TO
DIGITAL ETIQUETTE

KATHY FURGANG

rosen publishing's
rosen central

New York

To Adam

Published in 2011 by The Rosen Publishing Group, Inc.
29 East 21st Street, New York, NY 10010

Library of Congress Cataloging-in-Publication Data

Furgang, Kathy.
Netiquette: a student's guide to digital etiquette / Kathy Furgang. — 1st ed.
  p. cm. —(Digital and information literacy)
Includes bibliographical references and index.
ISBN 978-1-4358-9429-7 (library binding)
ISBN 978-1-4488-0597-6 (pbk)
ISBN 978-1-4488-0602-7 (6 pack)
1. Online etiquette—Juvenile literature. I. Title.
TK5105.878.F87 2011
395.5—dc22

2009048676

Manufactured in the United States of America

CPSIA Compliance Information: Batch #S10YA: For further information, contact Rosen Publishing, New York, New York, at 1-800-237-9932.

CONTENTS

INTRODUCTION

In our fast-paced digital age, we can find new gadgets to make life easier, including new Web sites to help us find just about anything imaginable. But one thing that has lagged behind this rapid digital advancement is an established way for people to behave online and when using new technologies. The word "etiquette" refers to the proper and polite way to behave in society. These unwritten rules of behavior provide guidance for how to act in various situations. For example, the rules of behavior are different in a school, at a party, or at a company meeting. Etiquette is a code of manners. It helps social activities run smoothly, and it makes the person following the rules of etiquette look good to others.

Digital etiquette, or netiquette, is very similar to the social rules we use in our everyday lives. Digital etiquette provides people with unwritten rules about how to behave while using personal technology devices. And the purpose is the same as traditional etiquette. Netiquette is meant to create a pleasant, safe, and civil environment for every member of the online community to enjoy. Our cities and towns depend on the good behavior of its citizens to make the environment safe. In the same way, our online communities depend on the good behavior of citizens to make the cyber environment safe. Just as you wouldn't break into a store in your neighborhood, you wouldn't hack into, or break into, a Web site. Just as you shouldn't gossip

Rules of behavior on the Internet and when using digital technology in public are similar to the "real world" social rules we follow every day.

rudely about a friend or acquaintance in a face-to-face conversation, you shouldn't talk behind someone's back or spread rumors in e-mails or on social networking sites.

The Internet is a public community. Just as we need to use manners in public, we also need to use manners while online. Whether conducting research for a school report or interacting with friends on a social networking site, it helps to know how to behave responsibly. When you interact with someone in a digital way, just remember that you are interacting with a real person, even though you cannot see him or her. Don't do or say anything that you wouldn't do or say in person. You are sharing digital space with millions of users. The Internet is a place people of all ages can visit. Some of these fellow users are your parents' or grandparents' age. Some are young children. You can help to make the cyber environment safe, pleasant, and enjoyable for everyone.

Digital etiquette refers to more than just speaking politely to people online. It is also concerned with the correct way to use computers and Internet access in public. In addition, netiquette refers to researching responsibly online, not stealing other people's work, and crediting sources correctly. Its principles should guide you when working on group projects in which you have access to other people's computers. Netiquette even extends to the use of cell phone calls and text messaging in school and other public places. Most of these guidelines for online and electronic etiquette are based on common sense and respect for others. Some online behavior is even governed by state or federal laws. The more you know about how to behave in a digital world, the more useful, safe, and enjoyable that world can be for you.

Chapter 1

Out in Public

ot everyone has a personal computer at home. Many students rely on the public computers in schools, libraries, and computer labs to get their work done and to correspond with friends over the Internet. If you are one of these people, you must be especially aware of the rules to follow when using computers that do not belong to you.

Using Public Computer Terminals

When using public computer terminals, there is often a limit to the amount of time you are allowed to spend using the workstation. Check around for posted rules. You will often find that you have to provide identification and enter your name on a sign-up sheet before being allowed to use the computer. This allows the library or computer lab that owns the computers to track who is using the different computer stations and who might be responsible for any problems that occur during the day.

Once you gain access to a computer terminal, you may have to log in with personal information such as your name, an identification number, or a

Rules for using public computers are different from using a computer at home. You should limit the amount of time you spend on a public computer and not use it for personal or private communication and Web surfing if other people are waiting to use it.

password. Do not give too much information. You should not be asked for a Social Security number or credit card number when using a public computer. Basic, public record information, such as your address or telephone number, should be enough information to identify you.

When you have followed all of the procedures necessary to begin using a public computer, you must then obey the time limits and the rules of the library or computer lab. Many libraries offer people a half hour to an hour of computer time per day. Others allow you to sign up again and wait at the end of the line for an additional session.

Sometimes, there are headphones available at the library, school, or computer lab. Be sure to use them if you are going to be listening to music, news reports, or other audio and video files and Web sites that use sound. The person next to you may be working on a difficult assignment and may be distracted by your noise.

There are often rules about downloading files on public computers. Sometimes you may be researching a topic for school and a Web site will require that you download a file onto your desktop to view it. However, check with the school, library, or computer lab workers to see if this is OK or if there is a designated place where you should be downloading these files instead. In addition, many public computers block the user from going to inappropriate Web sites.

Places that put no time limits on the use of their public computers rely on the user to limit him- or herself in order to allow everyone to have a turn. For example, if you are using a public computer to do a research report for school and you are finished with your work for the day, look around to see if people are waiting their turn for the computer. If there are people waiting for your terminal, don't start visiting Web pages that aren't work related or chatting with friends on social networking sites. Try to finish up your work and sign off on the computer so someone else can have a turn.

Using a Laptop in Public

Many people who have laptop computers enjoy using them in public places that offer Internet connections. It's very common to have free Wi-Fi, or wireless

WORK IN A WIRELESS AIRPORT

Wireless Internet service (Wi-Fi) allows people to get online when they are on the go. Today, you can be connected almost anywhere in the world, anytime.

Internet service, in libraries, hotels, stores, airports, or restaurants. The term "Wi-Fi" is an abbreviation for "wireless fidelity" and refers to wireless networking abilities that come from a device called a wireless router. The router broadcasts a signal through the air. The signal allows multiple devices to connect to the Internet with no need for wires or cables. The availability of these networks is becoming so common that it is easy to take your computer with you when you go out and quickly find a place that offers free Internet access.

Commonsense rules apply to using laptops in public places. Pay attention to any time limits placed on Wi-Fi users or any fees that apply (not all

File   Edit   View   Favorites   Tools   Help

      HISTORY OF CYBERCAFES

History of Cybercafes

A cybercafe is a café that, for a fee, offers Internet service either on computers that it owns or for laptop computers that customers bring into the café. Today, these specialized cafés are harder to find because we see Internet service everywhere we go—malls, coffee shops, libraries, hotels, airports, and bookstores. There is no longer as great a need for them as there once was.

The first cybercafe opened in London, England, in 1994. A cybercafe was a novelty then not because it served coffee and pastries but because it also sold Internet and computer access at a time when few people had their own computers and Internet connections, even at home. Eventually, as more people began to buy personal computers and could surf the Web at home, the cafés became a place travelers could check e-mail when away from home. Then laptops and Wi-Fi came along and revolutionized how and where people worked, communicated, and explored the Internet. Today, many ordinary cafés simply offer a free Wi-Fi connection to their customers.

Wi-Fi is free). Even when Wi-Fi connections are free, that does not mean you should take advantage of the place that is offering the service. Try not to take up more space than you need. Don't take over an entire table that paying customers may want to share. If you are in a café, order something to eat or drink. The café is in the business of selling food and drinks, not offering free Internet service. And bring some headphones if you are going to be playing music. The point is to be as discreet as possible when you are doing personal business in a public place. This refers not only to computer use but also to the use of cell phones and other digital and electronic technologies.

Use common sense when talking on a cell phone. The hustle and bustle of a noisy place makes it easier to talk without disturbing people around you. A library or movie theater, however, is a bad place to have a phone conversation.

Cell Phone and Texting Etiquette

A survey done in 2007 by America Online and the Associated Press reveals that 81 percent of the people surveyed were at least occasionally bothered by the use of cell phones in public places. Cell phones can be a great convenience for the user, but they can also be a major irritation for those around you.

If you receive a call in a public place, take note of the noise level where you are. If you're on a playground or at a sporting event, go ahead and chat away. But if you are in a bookstore, library, movie theater, or museum, take the call outside, let it go to voicemail, or tell the caller you will get back to him or her later. Chances are the caller doesn't realize where you are, so it's not rude to let him or her know that you can't talk. Also, your cell phone should be on silent or vibrate mode in these kinds of public places.

Texting can be an alternative form of communication in places where your speaking voice is not appreciated. Do not text in movie theaters or at plays, since the device's light distracts other audience members, as does the constant typing. Also, make sure you are not ignoring the people you are with when you do text. Many people view texting and talking on a cell phone as a sign of disrespect if the person they are out with does it too much. If you are in a restaurant with friends or family, think about turning your cell phone off or just replying to the texts later. The people you are with want to spend time with you and have your full attention.

For young people, forgoing texting or talking on their cell phones is sometimes hard to do. They have grown up with these technologies and do not view their use in social situations as annoying or rude. Many young people do not feel that they are being disrespected if a friend begins to talk to or text someone else when they are together. However, many other people do feel this way, and it is important to have respect for everyone around you.

Piggybacking

Most modern laptops are able to connect to the Internet without wires. This means that laptop owners can take their computers anywhere they go and more often than not find a place that offers access to the Internet via Wi-Fi. Before Wi-Fi, computers gained access to the Internet only through cable or phone line connections, making the computer immobile. People had to remain at their home, school, library, or office to do their work. Wi-Fi has allowed computers and their users to wander anywhere and gain Internet access in cafés, parks, hotel rooms and lobbies, trains, airports, and other public places.

Many coffee shops, restaurants, libraries, and bookstores now offer Wi-Fi, so Internet surfing via laptop, smart phones, and other mobile devices is quick, easy, and often free.

Before getting on the Internet via a public access Wi-Fi network, the user will have to check the computer's network settings to view and select from a list of connections available in the immediate area. These connections change as you move from place to place. If you are in your own home, for example, you may check your network settings and see your neighbors' Wi-Fi networks as well as your own. You may be at a café and see the names of wireless connections from nearby stores or businesses. Most of these will have a picture of a padlock next to them to indicate that access to that router is protected by a password. People do this to protect their privacy.

They paid for this connection and do not want strangers to log on to it and use it for free.

However, some people either do not know how to make their network private (password protected) or are not aware that it should be protected. Logging on to one of these unlocked Wi-Fi networks is called piggybacking. The person who has paid for his or her network connection is doing the digital equivalent of carrying you—that is, giving you a free ride. When you use this network without permission, you are stealing. In addition, when too many computers use one router signal, it can slow the connection for everyone.

So when you are out in public, choose only the free, unprotected networks that explicitly offer this Internet service to their customers. Some places that offer Internet access will have password protected networks, but they will provide you with the code or password to get online when you ask. This allows them to make sure that only their customers are using the service, not freeloading piggybackers.

Chapter 2

Researching Responsibly

The Internet is a great convenience when doing research for school projects. When students have a school report to write, they no longer have to rely exclusively on a library. Libraries may be difficult to get to or have inconvenient hours of operation and possibly outdated reference books that cannot be taken home. Now students can find accurate and reliable information online in the comfort of their own home.

Citing Sources and Avoiding Plagiarism

When learning how to research, organize, and write reports, you most likely learned about how to compile a bibliography or insert footnotes in your paper so that you can credit sources correctly. These same citation rules apply to information you get off the Internet. You can use Internet-derived information to get facts and data, but the sources must be cited. As is the case with printed books and articles, you cannot take exact wording off a Web site and place it in your report without making it clear that it is a quote and where it came from.

The Internet can make researching school papers quick and easy, but you must resist the urge to cut and paste someone else's text into your report without citing it.

According to an article in *USA Today*, students aren't using information technology responsibly. A study reveals that 83 percent of undergraduate college students use information technology (the Internet) for their academic work. However, close to 90 percent of these students admit that they have seen their peers "at least sometimes" copy and paste information from the Web without citing the source or paraphrasing the text (rewriting something in your own words). It may be easy to do with just the click of a finger, but it is not ethical and not legal according to copyright laws.

Copying and pasting will lead to more than just an unethical report. More and more students who use the Web as a way to get a lot of work done quickly admit that they are not truly learning or absorbing the content. Because the Internet is so fast and easy, students don't take the time to really sit down and understand what they are reading. It often takes time for your mind to absorb the information it is learning. Quickly skimming text and then cutting and pasting it into a report does nothing to further your understanding of the subject. This kind of research technique shows only that you knew how to find the information, not that you actually learned or understood it.

Students and Fair Use

Is simply citing the sources you use in your bibliography enough to allow you to use copyrighted information from Internet sources without seeking official permission? The fair use doctrine says it is enough. This copyright law is part of U.S. trademark law. It states that as long as the selection from the work you are reproducing is relatively short (like a quote), you do not have to get written permission from the copyright holder to use it. This especially applies to using materials for educational purposes. The rule of thumb is you may use 10 percent of a complete text or one thousand words, whichever is less. A song in a multimedia presentation can also be used without written permission from the copyright holder. Again, the rule of thumb is that 10 percent of a song's running time may be played or no more than thirty seconds. However, that material used should be listed in the project's bibliography. To avoid any confusion or legal trouble, however, it is always best to use public domain sources and materials or those that are specifically licensed for use under a Creative Commons license.

Audio and Video Files

Many people don't give much thought to how to credit audio and video files taken from the Web and used in presentations. But it is necessary to credit your sources no matter what kind of technology file they are. Suppose you are giving an oral multimedia presentation to your class. You want to

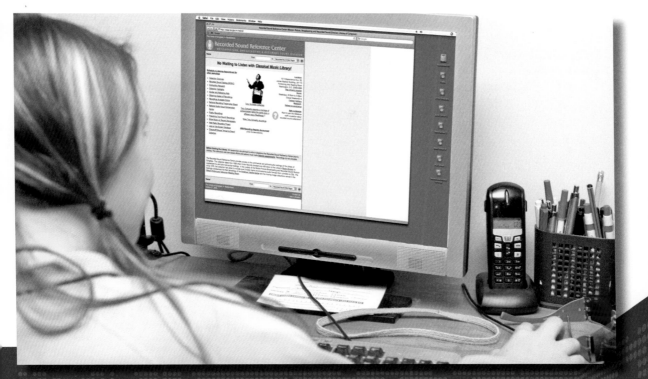

Adding downloaded audio or video files to your multimedia presentation can make it very dynamic and interesting, but be sure you observe all copyright laws and cite sources properly. Use public domain materials as much as possible.

use music in the background and you also want to project a video that you downloaded from a NASA Web site. You can certainly do all of these things. Just make a list of the materials used and the Web sites you got them from. Submit a complete list of sources to your teacher, including the material's title, the Web site's name, the date of the material's creation, the date you downloaded it, and the site's address, or URL.

Remember that in most cases you should not download songs from the Internet without paying for them. Most songs are protected by copyright laws. This means that the right to decide how a song gets used and distributed is up to the person who holds the copyright. In many cases, the artist holds the

The Library of Congress

AMERICAN MEMORY

Band Music from the Civil War Era

Music Division, Library of Congress

Search By Keyword | **Browse** Index of Subjects | Titles

Band Music from the Civil War Era makes available examples of a brilliant style of brass band music that flourished in the 1850s in the United States and remained popular through the nineteenth century. Bands of this kind served in the armies of both the North and the South during the Civil War. This online collection includes both printed and manuscript music (mostly in the form of "part books" for individual instruments) selected from the collections of the Music Division of the Library of Congress and the Walter Dignam Collection of the Manchester Historic Association (Manchester, New Hampshire). The collection features over 700 musical compositions, as well as 8 full-score modern editions and 19 recorded examples of brass band music in performance.

Legal and convenient archives of audio files have emerged in recent years. The Library of Congress (http://www.loc.gov) offers a rich trove of audio files—including music, speeches, and oral histories—for free download.

copyright and should receive payment when the works are downloaded and distributed over the Web. If you own a compact disc or MP3 file containing the music you want to use in your multimedia report, it is fine to use that in class. The CD has already been purchased, and you are not selling or distributing anything with the song on it. But you still must cite your sources by submitting a list of everything you have used in the creation of your presentation—books, magazines, Web articles, music files, video clips, and photos.

TEN GREAT QUESTIONS
TO ASK A DIGITAL LIBRARIAN

1. Why does my teacher make me use different media formats to give presentations in school?

2. How can I use a computer to give a presentation at school?

3. Is the information I get from the Internet better than the research I can get from books?

4. I do not have a computer at home, but I have a big research paper to do. How can I get extra time at a school computer?

5. My parents have not given me permission to use the Internet while I am at school, so I cannot do my research paper online. How else can I find digital information?

6. What should I do if the school blocks sites that I need to use in a report and I do not have a computer at home?

7. How can I save my research and work on my paper if I do not have a computer at home?

8. What should I do if I want to send my teacher a file, but he or she cannot open it?

9. How would someone know if the files I downloaded for a multimedia report were obtained legally or not?

10. How can I tell if the information I get off the Internet is accurate?

Chapter 3

A Group Effort

When using computers and digital technology for a group project, the members of the group must be careful to work respectfully with each other. Just as being in an office with coworkers requires following different behavioral rules than working alone does, the same goes for student groups.

If members of your group do research together, you may end up using each other's computers in the process of researching, compiling, and writing the report. Just keep in mind that a person's computer is a personal and private space. It should be treated as private property. Don't use your friend's or classmate's computer as your own. That includes not opening documents, changing computer settings, reading e-mails, viewing photos, or copying a person's files, such as music files, without permission.

E-mail Etiquette

When communicating online about a school report, keep it professional. Your teacher may ask to see your progress and sources. Imagine how it

Research for group projects requires that everyone does his or her fair share and respects each member of the group, both in face-to-face meetings and virtual communications.

would look if those sources were embedded in an e-mail to a group member that also discussed your favorite TV show, last night's football game, or trouble with a boyfriend or girlfriend.

As you write your e-mails regarding the group project, think about whom you are referring to in your correspondence. Are you mentioning any other students in the group? Be sure to carbon copy, or Cc, any other person you are talking about in your e-mail. This ensures that you will be careful and diplomatic regarding what you say about that person. It also keeps group members informed about your progress on the project. Don't refer to the other team members in a negative way, especially behind their

```
●●●                                    Hello                                      ▭

◁          ◯          ✎          🖼          A          ◉          🗂
Send      Chat      Attach    Address    Fonts     Colors   Save As Draft

       To: Johndoe@gmail.com

       Cc: CindyDoe@gmail.com, SusanDoe@hotmail.com

      Bcc:

  Subject: Hello

≡▾                                                        Signature:  None      ▴▾

Dear John Doe,
```

Today, e-mail often takes the place of letters that people once sent through the mail. Yet formal correspondence via e-mail should be written just like a proper letter—no slang, no abbreviations or emoticons, and no sentence fragments.

backs. Remember, you may be asked to show all your work on the project, including correspondence. It may be embarrassing for you and hurtful to the other student to see e-mails about a school project that portray him or her in a negative way.

The Rules of Official or Business Correspondence

Sometimes when working on a school project, you may want to correspond with someone from the community. Suppose you want to interview a local

File   Edit   View   Favorites   Tools   Help

CC ME!

Cc Me!

The abbreviation Cc stands for "carbon copy." It originated in the days before computers and photocopiers, when offices were not yet "paperless." When people typed letters on their typewriters and wanted to send copies to different people, they often used a piece of carbon paper. These purple carbon sheets were placed between two pieces of typing paper and rolled into the typewriter. When someone typed on the original top sheet, an exact copy was printed on the second sheet beneath the carbon paper. The original copy would go to the person the letter was addressed to, and the carbon copy went to others not addressed in the letter. Anyone who received a carbon copy would be listed on the bottom of the letter, after the initials Cc.

E-mail allows a further wrinkle. The Bcc option on e-mail address lines stands for "blind cc." That means that a person receives a copy of the e-mail, but none of the other recipients are aware that he or she has been sent it. The person's name and e-mail address do not show up in the address fields.

businessperson for a social studies, civics, or economics paper. Or maybe you want to invite a firefighter or a scientist to speak to your class as part of your project. You can talk with these people online and have a written record of the correspondence available for your teacher. This will help him or her better evaluate your work on the project and your level of involvement and commitment to its success. There are some simple rules about using proper digital etiquette when conducting professional (nonpersonal) correspondence via e-mail.

○ ○ ○   Hello ⬭

Send   Chat   Attach   Address   Fonts   Colors   Save As Draft

To: KellyL@gmail.com

Cc:

Bcc:

Subject: Hello

≡▾   Signature: None ▾

Hey,
How R U? It was GR8 seeing U.
R we still meeting up 2morrow?

Call u LTR.
:-)

Using abbreviations and e-mail shorthand with friends in personal correspondence is fine. But if you want to be taken seriously by a teacher, business professional, college admissions officer, or other adult, you must compose e-mails that are formal, respectful, and grammatically correct.

Just like a formal letter that is printed on paper, nonpersonal e-mail correspondence should have a greeting, a body, and a conclusion. The e-mail will show the date, so you do not need to include that in the body of your letter. Your e-mail should not include any Internet shorthand or abbreviated spellings. Abbreviations such as btw for "by the way," or PLMK for "please let me know," are OK between friends. But they are not appropriate in a business e-mail. When writing e-mails, people often don't use correct punctuation, spelling, or capitalization. Yet this, too, is inappropriate for a business letter or a letter to someone you do not know well.

In addition to writing the letter in a professional manner, you must also give the person enough time to respond. If you are asking the person to visit your classroom or be interviewed next week, be sure to send the e-mail as soon as possible. Not everyone checks e-mail every day, so you want to give the person time to read your message and consider the offer. It would be insulting if you e-mailed someone asking him or her to give a talk the next day or even the day after tomorrow. People have busy lives and their time is valuable, so be respectful and give them plenty of advance notice.

Your letter should also provide as much information as possible about the project and what you hope the interviewee can contribute to it so he or she does not need to ask you a lot of questions. If the person does not respond within a couple of days, send a friendly follow-up letter. If you are turned down, send a polite thank-you e-mail for the person's time and consideration. Keep in mind that you may need a backup plan for your project if the person is unable to help. If you get a favorable response, be sure to thank the person for his or her time and effort both before and after participation.

Crediting Your Group's Sources

When you are writing the bibliography for a project you did with a group, look at each source. Think about whether you actually used that book as a source of information. Did you do the research, or did another person in your group do it? If the project has a group credit, which means it was researched and written by the whole group, it may be OK if you are not familiar with all the sources that were referred to and used. But if you are responsible for writing your own paper, you should know exactly how and when you used each source that appears in the bibliography.

One of the things you should include in your bibliography is the date that you accessed each Internet article. You may find that another person in your group used the same article, but he or she may have accessed it on a different day. Some Web sites are updated daily or weekly, so your partner may have downloaded a revised article or one that was not as recent and current as yours. Be as accurate as you can with your recordkeeping.

MYTHS & FACTS

MYTH What I do online is my own private business.

FACT There are laws regarding Internet use. It is never OK to harass someone. Laws regarding harassment apply to digital correspondence. And if you delete an e-mail in an effort to remove traces of it, it is possible that the person you sent the message to may have already reported you to an authority.

MYTH Cyber bullying only happens when someone threatens to hurt someone else and it can only happen on social networking sites.

FACT Insults and put-downs are also considered cyber bullying. Calling someone names online, even a friend, is considered bullying. It can happen in e-mails or text messages, or through social networking sites.

MYTH If I tell an adult that I am being cyber bullied, the whole situation will get even worse.

FACT Most cyber bullying of children is ended with the help of adults. Parents, teachers, and even the police can step in and help the person who is being bullied.

Chapter 4

Netiquette at Home

After using school computers to do project research online, many students go home and face the most important challenge of digital etiquette—personal Internet use. Not all teens are monitored by their parents when they get on the computer. They can sometimes begin interacting with people online in a way that is not safe or appropriate.

It is important to understand the rules of digital etiquette in order to remain safe from very real trouble in the so-called virtual world. Being familiar with digital etiquette will also help you recognize when someone is not following these important rules and trying to get you into trouble. These people should be avoided. When someone is not following the rules, it is important to let an adult know.

Here are some of the most common, and also the most dangerous, ways that people take advantage of the anonymity offered by the Internet, use poor netiquette, and victimize individual computer users within the cyber community.

Lori Drew *(center)* arrives at court during her trial for cyberbullying. She was accused of creating a fake MySpace page to harass Megan Meier, her daughter Sarah's *(left)* former friend. Megan killed herself when the phony MySpace romance orchestrated by Drew turned ugly.

Cyber Bullying

Cyber bullying is the use of digital technologies to express deliberate, repeated, and hostile behavior toward others. It can happen through e-mail, text messages, instant messages, blogs, or chat rooms in a private or public format. Social networking sites such as Facebook, Twitter, and MySpace have become places where bullying occasionally occurs among students and other young people.

Cyber bullying is more common than you may think. According to a survey by *USA Today*, nearly half of all teenagers say that they have been victims of some kind of cyber bullying. Those numbers may be even higher since many teens and young people are afraid to admit and report that they are being harassed. They may feel that their problems will get worse if they tell someone and draw attention to it. Sometimes they are embarrassed that they are being targeted or that people may not like them. But the best way to stop a problem is to address it directly and do something about it. Do not continue to talk to the bully, either in person or via electronic communication. It is important to involve a trusted adult in the problem.

Even minor cases of cyber bullying can affect a person's well-being, making it difficult to go online, concentrate, or even study or do homework. Severe cases of cyber bullying have led to criminal attacks, and in several cases, it has even led to the suicide of the bullying victim.

E-mailing and Posting Personal and Inappropriate Content

Some people send photos or videos of themselves to friends. These images are meant for their friends' eyes only and may not be something they'd want anyone else to see. They may also send e-mails that are very private in nature or tell off-color jokes. Though meant as an inside joke or to be amusing in a private way, these images and words would be inappropriate if they somehow were viewed by someone other than the intended recipient. Other people, including classmates and strangers, may get their hands on these words and images, spread them around, and misuse them.

Many young people do not realize that once their images and words are sent, the digital information can be passed on or posted over the Internet to a large group of people without permission. Many times, students do not realize that, although they may trust their friend now, it

Be careful of the information you share with others in texts or e-mails. It may come back to haunt you if a friendship sours or the wrong person gets his or her hands on the information and spreads it.

is possible that they may not be able to trust him or her in the future. In addition, the inappropriate depiction of people below the age of eighteen in photos or on video is illegal. This type of depiction is called child pornography.

Also, be cautious about posting overly personal, private, or inappropriate content on your blog, Web site, or social networking site. Not only do you have limited control (at best) over who can view this material, it will also continue to exist on the Web long after you post it—and probably long after you come to regret it. This means that future boyfriends or girlfriends, college admissions officers, employers, and law enforcement and government agents will all be able to find this content if they wish to conduct a search on you for any reason. Once you put it out there, it's very hard, if not impossible, to reel it back in. A good rule of thumb is not to post any images or words that you wouldn't want your grandparents, future in-laws, or future boss to see.

Internet Predators

An Internet predator is someone who uses e-mail, dating sites, online classifieds, social networking sites, and Web portals to make contact with

Texas attorney general Greg Abbott stands before a poster displaying some of the three hundred predators captured by the state's fugitive and cyber-crime units.

people for the purpose of harming them. A predator may want to rob, deceive, abduct, or attack a person physically or sexually. One in five teenagers in the United States who use the Internet regularly say that they have received unwanted sexual offers online. This means someone has contacted them without invitation and tried to talk about sex or arrange a face-to-face meeting to have sex. Unfortunately, only 25 percent of these

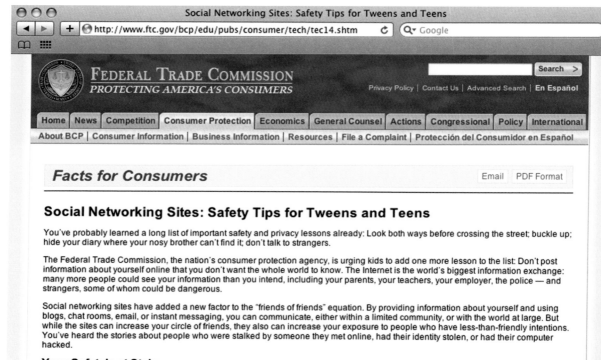

Online interaction can become dangerous. Government Web sites, like that of the Federal Trade Commission (http://www.ftc.gov), help alert computer users to the dangers.

teens told a parent or trusted adult about it. Internet predators have been responsible for abductions, murders, and sexual crimes. They are also often skilled at seduction, luring confused and lonely teens into inappropriate sexual relationships.

To avoid Internet predators, never talk to people online that you do not know. Never give away personal information to anyone, including your name, address, phone number, or other identifying data. From the safe invisibility of the keyboard, Internet predators often present themselves as someone your own age or as someone who is a friend of a friend of yours. They may even impersonate someone you know and trust. You must always remain vigilant when communicating on the Internet and not be taken in by predators and imposters. If you make a date to meet a friend or acquaintance via e-mail, Facebook, or text messaging, be sure to confirm with a phone call so you know for sure that you've been communicating with the real person and not someone posing as him or her.

Flaming

The word "flaming" refers to the hostile or insulting interactions that people can have on the Internet. People tend to say things on the Internet that they wouldn't feel comfortable saying in person. People tend to feel more comfortable expressing anger, disgust, or disapproval in written form over the Internet. Leaving comments on someone's Facebook, MySpace, or Twitter page that are rude or insulting is not good netiquette.

People often engage in flaming on blogs, chat rooms, message boards, or other sites where people are invited to post reviews of consumer products, music, movies, or books. Strangers can get into arguments in these discussion threads, with an unlimited number of people able to view them. Sometimes, once an aggressive user attacks someone who has posted a comment he or she disagrees with, other users feel emboldened to join in and gang up on the flaming victim.

Flaming is a mean-spirited, aggressive, and antisocial Internet behavior that is designed only to intimidate, shock, and anger people. Avoid these kinds of toxic virtual conversations and report any flamer you encounter online.

Even if you have a user name that does not reveal your real name—and you should choose a nonidentifying user name—this kind of harassment can make the Internet an unpleasant place for everyone. It can make people hesitant to express an opinion, engage in intelligent and heartfelt conversation, or even venture onto the Internet at all. The atmosphere created by flamers is very much like that created by schoolyard bullies. They turn what should be supportive and stimulating environments into ones poisoned by anger, dread, intimidation, fear, and, ultimately, silence. Just as you would try to be civil to a person you talk with in person, have the same kind of respect for people online.

Do not hide behind the idea that what you are posting is anonymous because people do not know you or your real name. Think about what you are posting. Would you be willing to deliver this message to the person face-to-face? We must all do our part to create a safe and welcoming cyber community. Just as you would try to be a good neighbor in your town or in your school, it is also your responsibility to be a good citizen in cyberspace. Think about whether the statement you are posting is something you would like to read about yourself. If you are in an argument with a friend, think twice before you post something nasty on his or her Facebook page. Just think of what it would be like for all of your friends, family, classmates, and acquaintances to read unflattering things about you on your personal page.

The Golden Rule of Netiquette

Keep in mind this ancient and ever reliable recommendation, as relevant in the twenty-first century as it was in the first century: do unto others as you would have them do unto you. All of the principles and guidelines of netiquette—as they relate to public use of computers and electronic devices, academic research, group projects, and business and personal communication—are encapsulated in this timeless Golden Rule. It will always steer you right, whether in the real world or the virtual universe that is the World Wide Web.

GLOSSARY

bibliography A list of books or other information sources used in a report.

blog Short for "Web log"; a Web site in which an ongoing, often personal, narrative is written and archived by a single author.

Cc A carbon copy; an exact copy of a message or letter sent to a person who is not the addressee or primary recipient of the letter.

chat room A place on the Internet where groups of people can communicate together in real time. Chat rooms are usually organized around and devoted to a specific subject, topic, or interest.

copyright The legal right to publish works or perform art, and the right to allow others to do so.

cyber bullying Using digital technologies to express deliberate, repeated, and hostile behaviors toward others.

cybercafe A café that offers Internet access to its customers, usually for a fee.

digital etiquette Unwritten rules about how to behave while using personal technology devices.

download To copy a file or program from one computer system and move it to another computer system for use there.

etiquette The polite way to behave in society.

fair use doctrine A U.S. law that states that copyright material may be used without permission or payment as long the quoted material is brief.

file sharing The ability to transmit or share files over the Internet or over computer networks.

flaming The hostile or insulting interactions that people can have on the Internet.

instant messaging An exchange of online messages between two or more people sent in real time.

Internet predator Someone who uses e-mails or Web sites to reach people for the purpose of doing harm to them.

netiquette The manners used while working online.

piggybacking Logging on to an unauthorized Wi-Fi network.

plagiarism Using someone else's words or work as your own without citing or attributing your source.

pornography The inappropriate or obscene depiction of people in a sexual way.

router Computer hardware that allows a networked computer to access the Internet without connection via a cable or telephone line; it allows a computer user to access the Internet in a wireless manner from any location that is in range of the router.

social networking The practice of reaching out and staying in touch with others; in this context, the term used to describe the communication of many people for social purposes via the Internet.

texting A written, digital correspondence sent by cell phone signals.

Wi-Fi Wireless Internet service.

FOR MORE INFORMATION

Canadian Centre for Child Protection
615 Academy Road
Winnipeg, MB R3N 0E7
Canada
(204) 945-5735
(800) 532-9135
Web sites: http://www.protectchildren.ca/app/en
             http://www.cybertip.ca/app/en
The Canadian Centre for Child Protection is a nonprofit, charitable
    organization dedicated to the personal safety of all children. Its goal is
    to reduce child victimization by providing programs and services
    to the Canadian public. It operates Cybertip.ca, Canada's national
    tipline for reporting online sexual exploitation of children. It is part
    of the national government's efforts to make Canada safer for
    its citizens.

Family Online Safety Institute
815 Connecticut Avenue, Suite 220
Washington, DC, 20006
(202) 572-6252
Web site: http://www.fosi.org
The Family Online Safety Institute is an international, nonprofit organization
    that works to make the Internet safe for children and families. It works to
    influence public policies and educate the public.

Internet Education Foundation
1634 I Street NW, Suite 1100
Washington, DC, 20006
(202) 637-0968

Web site: http://neted.org
The Internet Education Foundation is a nonprofit organization dedicated to
    informing the public about Internet education.

i-Safe
5900 Pasteur Court, Suite 100
Carlsbad, CA 92008
(760) 603-7911
Web site: http://www.isafe.org
Founded in 1998, i-SAFE is a nonprofit foundation whose mission is to
    educate and empower youth to make their Internet experiences safe
    and responsible. The goal is to educate students on how to avoid
    dangerous, inappropriate, or unlawful online behavior.

National Center for Missing & Exploited Children (NCMEC)
Charles B. Wang International Children's Building
699 Prince Street
Alexandria, VA 22314-3175
(703) 224-2150
(800) The-LOST (843-5678)
Web site: http://www.netsmartz.org/index.aspx
The NCMEC'S mission is to help prevent child abduction and sexual
    exploitation, help find missing children, and assist victims of child
    abduction and sexual exploitation, their families, and the professionals
    who serve them. The NCMEC operates both the CyberTipline and
    NetSmartz.org (tips for families, children, and teens about online safety).

Safe Canada
Attn: Public Safety Portal—SafeCanada.ca

269 Laurier Avenue
West Ottawa, ON K1A 0P8
Canada
(800) 755-7047
Web site: http://www.safecanada.ca/topic_e.asp?category=3
Safe Canada is part of the Canadian government's online efforts to make
      Canada a safe place for all its citizens wherever they are—including
      when they visit cyberspace.

Web Sites

Due to the changing nature of Internet links, Rosen Publishing has developed
an online list of Web sites related to the subject of this book. This site is
updated regularly. Please use this link to access this list:

http://www.rosenlinks.com/dil/neti

FOR FURTHER READING

Appleman, Dan. *Always Use Protection: A Teen's Guide to Safe Computing.* New York, NY: Apress, 2004.

Bailey, Diane. *Cyber Ethics.* New York, NY: Rosen Central, 2008.

Furgang, Adam. *Searching Online for Image, Audio, and Video Files* (Digital and Information Literacy). New York, NY: Rosen Publishing, 2009.

Gaines, Ann. *Ace Your Internet Research* (Ace It! Information Literacy Series). Berkeley Heights, NJ: Enslow Publishers, 2009.

Goodstein, Anastasia. *Totally Wired: What Teens and Tweens Are Really Doing Online.* New York, NY: St. Martin's Griffin. 2007.

Hawthorn, Kate. *A Young Person's Guide to the Internet.* New York, NY: Routledge, 2005.

Post Senning, Cindy. *Teen Manners: From Malls to Meals to Messaging and Beyond.* New York, NY: HarperCollins, 2007.

Shaw, Maura D. *Mastering Online Research.* Cincinnati, OH: Writer's Digest Books, 2007.

Sommers, Michael. *The Dangers of Online Predators.* New York, NY: Rosen Central, 2008.

Willard, Nancy. *Cyber-Safe Kids, Cyber-Savvy Teens.* New York, NY: Jossey-Bass, 2007.

BIBLIOGRAPHY

ABC News. "Parents: Cyber Bullying Led to Teen's Suicide." ABCNews. com, November 19, 2007. Retrieved September 2009 (http:// abcnews.go.com/GMA/story?id=3882520&page=1).

Brain, Marshall, and Tracy V. Wilson. "How WiFi Works." HowStuffWorks.com. Retrieved September 19, 2009 (http:// computer.howstuffworks.com/wireless-network.htm).

Cox, Amy. "Where Are Your High-Tech Manners?" CNN.com, July 3, 2007. Retrieved October 5, 2009 (http://www.cnn.com/2007/ TECH/ptech/07/01/la.tech.manners/index.html?iref=newssearch).

Dean, Katie. "School Blocks Out File-Trading." *Wired*, May 2, 2003. Retrieved May 14, 2009 (http://www.wired.com/entertainment/ music/news/2003/05/58698).

i-Safe. "Cyber Bullying: Statistics and Tips." iSafe.org. Retrieved October 10, 2009 (http://www.isafe.org/channels/sub.php?ch=op&sub_id= media_cyber_bullying).

Kallos, Judith. *E-mail Etiquette Made Easy*. Raleigh, NC: Lulu.com, 2007.

Marklein, Mary Beth. "Students Aren't Using Info Technology Responsibly." *USA Today*, November 9, 2003. Retrieved May 14, 2009 (http://www.usatoday.com/news/education/2003-11-09- students-it_x.htm).

Martin, Jennifer. "$1.9 Million Verdict for Illegal Music Downloads." *Commercial Law*, August 1, 2009. Retrieved October 5, 2009 (http://ucclaw.blogspot.com/2009/06/19-million-verdict-for- illegal-music.html).

Sentry PC. "Shocking Statistics." SentryPC.com. Retrieved October 10, 2009 (http://www.sentrypc.com/statistics.htm).

Shea, Virginia. "The Core Rules of Netiquette." Albion.com. Retrieved May 14, 2009 (http://www.albion.com/netiquette/corerules.html).

Shipley, David, and Will Schwalbe. *Send: Why People E-mail So Badly and How to Do It Better.* Revised ed. New York, NY: Borzoi Books, 2008.

Steele, Jeffrey. *Email: The Manual: Everything You Should Know About E-mail Etiquette, Policies, and Legal Liability Before You Hit Send.* Portland, OR: Marion Street Press, Inc., 2006.

Strawbridge, Matthew. *Netiquette: Internet Etiquette in the Age of the Blog.* Ely, England: Software Reference, Ltd., 2006.

Swartz, Jon. "Schoolyard Bullies Get Nastier Online." *USA Today*, March 6, 2005. Retrieved October 5, 2009 (http://www.usatoday.com/tech/news/2005-03-06-cover-cyberbullies_x.htm).

Vaisman, Mauro. "Facebook, Twitter, and Online Bullying." *BusinessWeek*, March 24, 2009. Retrieved October 5, 2009 (http://www.businessweek.com/careers/workingparents/blog/archives/2009/03/facebook_twitte.html).

Willard, Nancy. *Cyberbullying and Cyberthreats: Responding to the Challenge of Online Social Aggression, Threats, and Distress.* Champaign, IL: Research Press, 2007.

INDEX

A

audio files, crediting, 18–19, 20

B

bibliographies, 16, 18, 27

C

cafes, using computers in, 11
"Cc," 25
cell phones, using in public, 6, 11, 12–13
child pornography, 32
computers
    laptop, 9–11, 13
    using friends', 22
    using public, 7–9
copyright laws, 18, 19
cyber bullying, 28, 30–31
cybercafes, history of, 11

D

digital librarian, questions to ask a, 21
downloading files to public computers, 9

E

e-mail etiquette, 22–24
etiquette, definition of, 4

F

fair use, 18
flaming, 35–37

G

Golden Rule of netiquette, 37
group projects, 6, 22–27

H

headphones, using, 9, 11
home, Internet use at, 29–37

I

inappropriate content
    in e-mails, 31–32
    on the Internet, 32–33

L

laptop, using in public, 9–11, 13
laws, and Internet use, 6, 28

M

music, paying for downloaded, 19–20

N

netiquette
    definition of, 4, 6
    Golden Rule of, 37
    at home, 29–37
    myths and facts about, 28
    in public, 6, 7–15
    purpose of, 4–6

About the Author

Kathy Furgang has been writing books for students for more than ten years. She has written more than twenty books for children and teens, including nonfiction books about science and technology. She worked for eight years as an editor of science textbooks for children and teachers. She lives in upstate New York with her husband and two sons.

Photo Credits

Cover, p. 1 (left), p. 32 © www.istockphoto.com/Sean Locke; cover, p. 1 (second from left), p. 36 © www.istockphoto.com/Ryan Lane; cover, p. 1 (second from right), p. 23 © www.istockphoto.com/Zsolt Nyulaszi; cover, p. 1 (right), p. 19 © www.istockphoto.com/Robert Hadfield; cover (background), interior graphics © www.istockphoto.com; p. 5 © Antonio Mo/Getty Images; p. 8 © Yellow Dog Productions/Getty Images; p. 10 © agefotostock/Getty Images; p. 12 © Altrendo Images/Getty Images; p. 14 © Thomas Northcut/Getty Images; p. 17 © Shutterstock; p. 20 Library of Congress; p. 30 © Jonathan Alcott/Zuma Press; p. 33 © AP Images.

Designer: Nicole Russo; Photo Researcher: Marty Levick